CHRISTIAN CREDIT DEVELOPMENT

THE 7-DAY CREDIT REPAIR & FINANCIAL FREEDOM PUBLICATION

DR. MICHAEL W. COUCH

Christian Credit Development: The 7-Day Credit Repair & Financial Freedom Publication

www.drmikecouch.com

Printed in the United States of America

ISBN: 978-1-7359185-4-9 (Paperback)

ISBN: 978-1-7359185-5-6 (Ebook)

CONTENTS

ADVANCED PRAISE

Dr. Couch,

It's been a pleasure working with you. I've had the opportunity to learn and embrace the skills it takes to budget and maintain an above-average credit score. I look forward to purchasing my home in the next two years.

Your services were extraordinary and I greatly appreciated them.

Sincerely,

Ms. F. Ellzy

Director of Marketing & Communication

To Whom It May Concern:

I met Dr. Couch approximately three years ago through a friend who told me that their new financial advisor could help me improve my credit score. At that time in my life, I was desperate and my credit score was around 325!

Three years later after following what I called *"Dr. Couch road to credit recovery doctrine"*, I have major credit cards such as American Express, a major bank issued me a secure loan that I paid off and purchase my first home. During these three years, I followed the doctrine about 75 percent of the time, and then the rest I cause some bumps in the road to credit recovery.

I recommend Dr. Couch as an excellent financial advisory because I am living proof of what you can accomplish by following his lead!

Sincerely,

Mr. C. Richardson

Manager - Natural Gas Services

INTRODUCTION

> *"After this manner, therefore, pray ye: Our Father which art in heaven, Hallowed be thy name. Thy Kingdom come. Thy will be done in earth, as it is in heaven. Give us this day our daily bread. And lead us not into temptation, but deliver us from evil: For thine is the kingdom, and the power, and the glory, forever. Amen."*
>
> — *Matthew 6:9-13 (KJV)*

Since Creation, man has suffered from his own greed and inability to obey God. In the Garden of Eden, Adam and Eve disobeyed God and were cast out to earn their own way. In Genesis 3:19 (ESV) , God said, *"By the sweat of your face you shall eat bread."* Until Christ returns, man will be concerned with acquiring and managing possessions.

You now belong to a select group of believers that Elohim has empowered. Who has decided to stop being victims of the credit and financial system and become credit and financially conscious believers that believe in the Lord Jesus Christ our Savior?

It is important to understand that you should not apply for any credit until you have completed the basic steps in restoring your credit and financial health. Please remember that no credit file and financial woes are beyond rebuilding. Philippians 4:13 (KJV) *"I can do all things through Christ which strengtheneth me."*

You must prioritize obtaining your credit report, removing or minimizing unfavorable credit entries, and adding new favorable credit references. Establishing and maintaining a good credit history and a stable financial future is vital to your ministry and your family's success.

WHAT IS THE PURPOSE OF CREDIT?

Credit allows you to purchase things you want now and pay for them later. This is good if you buy what you can afford. This is not good if you are buying things that you cannot afford. This basic rule of thumb applies to purchasing a house or buying a gift for someone. Purchase what you can afford.

You must use your own judgment and your wisdom of your own financial situation to decide when and how to use credit. Credit card companies make money by allowing you to use their money to buy something now. They are not doing you a favor. In fact, department stores, credit card companies, and mortgage companies would not lend you money if they did not make money. These companies base their decision on what the credit report looks like, such as "credit score." The borrower must carefully decide when they want to pay a company to allow them to use their money.

What Is In Your Credit File?

A credit report includes information on all your accounts, payments you have made on time or that are overdue, the balances on loans, lines of credit, credit cards, and any unpaid debts. Codes are used to show if the account is current "all payments are up to date, overdue, one or more payments is owed, or charge off, or never paid." A sheet explaining these codes is included with the report.

The following five things are what you should look for in your credit file:

- **IDENTIFICATION** - includes Social Security number(s), present and previous addresses, P.O. Boxes, phone numbers, and employment information.
- **CREDIT HISTORY** - information on all previous and present credit accounts with rating codes.
- **INQUIRIES** - all businesses who have checked your credit.
- **PUBLIC RECORDS** - any bankruptcies, judgments, or liens.
- **CONSUMER STATEMENT** - a 100-word response from you to any item in the report.

HOW DO I GET A COPY OF MY CREDIT REPORT?

You can get your credit report from www.MyFico.com or by requesting it from three major credit bureaus separately online or by phone. Please visit these websites to educate yourself and maximize the tools that they have to offer.

Experian	TransUnion	Equifax
701 Experian Parkway Allen, TX 75013	P.O. Box 2000 Chester, PA 19022-2000	P.O. Box 105167 Atlanta, GA 30374
888-397-3742	800-888-4213	800-685-1111
www.experian.com	www.transunion.com	www.equifax.com

Canadians can also get their credit reports online:

Equifax Canada	TransUnion Canada	Northern Credit Bureaus, Inc
www.equifax.com (Click on the "Canada" link)	www.tuc.ca	www.creditbureau.ca

Request your free credit reports:

Annual Credit Report.com

Central Source LLC

P.O. Box 105283

Atlanta, GA 30348-5283

877-322-8228

https://www.annualcreditreport.com

What should you do if you find a mistake in your credit file?

If there are items on the report that you are disputing. You should document everything you do when handling your request to have items removed from your credit report. Keep in mind that all negative items in your credit file should not be there longer than seven years. If the items remain longer than that, you have the right to dispute the information and have the information removed. Innovis can help with disputes and so much more. You can review their services and all the ways they can help at www.innovis.com. You can dispute any inaccurate information online with the credit bureaus through their website, or you can use an investigation letter by mail.

You have the right to dispute anything in your credit file. Please visit: "The Fair Credit Reporting Act" https://www.consumer.ftc.gov

**INVESTIGATION LETTER
(SAMPLE)**

Credit Bureau Name:
Address:
City, State. Zip Code:

Your Name:
Address:
City, State. Zip Code:
Your Social Security#:
Your D.O.B:

To Whom It May Concern:

I am requesting that the items listed below be immediately investigated. These inaccuracies are most injurious to my credit history.

Name of the Company	Account#	Dollar Amount
ABC's Company	56789000000	$30,879.00
DEF's Company	12340909090	$15,987.00
GHI's Company	987654321	$5,098.00

Please forward me an updated credit report after you have completed your credit investigation.

Your prompt attention and cooperation in this matter are greatly appreciated.

Sincerely,

(Your name goes here)

Tips for sending your letter to the credit bureaus:

- Make a copy of your Driver License or State ID
- Make a copy of your Social Security Card
- Make a copy of your Investigation Letter for your file
- Send by Certified Mail/Priority Mail (tracking#)

HOW TO BUILD CREDIT?

- Pay your monthly rent https://www.experian.com/rentbureau/rental-payment and utilities on time by adding them to your credit report. https://www.experian.com/consumer-products/score-boost.html
- Open, use and maintain a checking account responsibly "no bad checks."
- Start a savings account and make regular deposits that earn interest, such as Certificate of Deposit "CD" or Individual Retirement Account "IRA."
- Set up a budget and live with it.
- Use personal identification consistently.
- Pay off accounts in collections.
- Reducing your credit card balance will boost your FICO score.
- Get a secured credit card.
- Become an authorized user.
- Request a credit limit increase.
- https://www.transunion.com/savings/creditCard
- https://www.ucesprotectionplan.com/Default.aspx?rid=MCouch

THE 7-DAY FINANCIAL FREEDOM OUTLINE

Day One:

What is your financial goal?

Examples:

- New Home, New Car, $1,000,000 in your mutual fund account, retire you and your wife at the age of 35.
- https://www.kiplinger.com/personal-finance
- https://www.collegesavings.org

Day Two:

What is your budget for today, the week, the month, and the year?

In other words, what you do today will equal your year?

Examples:

- Daily income ($100 a day), daily expenses (food, gas, snacks, Starbucks, etc.)
- https://www.crown.org/
- https://www.moneysupermarket.com/saving

Day Three:

What is your debt amount?

Start with the lowest balance first and work to pay it off quickly. Once it is paid off, cut up the card(if it is a credit card), but don't close the account. For a house or a car, send a little extra to the principal every month.

Examples:

- Name of Creditor, interest rate, and amount owed
- https://www.marketwatch.com
- https//www.ratecity.com

Day Four:

What is your investment plan for retirement?

Amount Invested - Current Value - Years to Availability - Goal Amount

Examples:

- IRAs do provide the option of saving up to 3,000 per year and allow the money to grow without taxes: 401k, 403b, 457, IRA, SEP-IRA, KEOGH, Annuity, and others.

- https://www.treasurydirect.gov
- https://www.ssa.gov/

Day Five:

What are the insurances you have?

Examples:

- Life - Health - Homeowner's or Renter's - Auto
- Policy Type - Annual Premium - Detail of Coverage
- If you have economic dependents, you need to have life insurance to support your family. If you earn $50,000.00 each year, you will purchase between $420,000 and $500,000 of term life.
- https://selectquote.com/
- https://insurancestep.com/quote

Day Six:

What is your Estate Plan?

Example:

- Last Will and Testament - Disinheriting - Prenuptial Agreements - Trust
- https://www.nolo.com/
- https://couchm.wearelegalshield.com/

Day Seven:

What is your second source of income?

Example:

- Second Job - Home Business - Extra money can affect your financial health
- $500 per month invested in the stock market, averaging 11 percent per year, would be worth $227,000 in just 15 years!
- Having a 15-year mortgage for $150,000 with an 8 percent interest rate and you paid an extra $500 per month, you would pay off the entire mortgage in only nine years!
- https://www.fiverr.com/
- https://www.indeed.com/

GOD'S PROMISES FOR FINANCIAL FREEDOM

"To the person who pleases him, God gives wisdom, knowledge and happiness, but to the sinner he gives the task of gathering and storing up wealth to hand it over to the one who pleases God. This too is meaningless, a chasing after the wind." (Ecclesiastes 2:26 NIV)

"Ship your grain across the sea; after many days you may receive a return. Invest in seven ventures, yes, in eight; you do not know what disaster may come upon the land. If clouds are full of water, they pour rain on the earth. Whether a tree falls to the south or to the north, in the place where it falls, there it will lie. Whoever watches the wind will not plant; whoever looks at the clouds will not reap. As you do not know the path of the wind, or how the body is formed in a mother's womb, so you cannot understand the work of God, the Maker of all things. Sow your seed in the morning, and at evening let your hands not be idle, for you do not know which will succeed, whether this or that, or whether both will do equally well." (Ecclesiastes 11:1-6 NIV)

"Celebrate the Festival of Unleavened Bread; for seven days eat bread made without yeast, as I commanded you. Do this at the appointed time in the month of Aviv, for in that month you came out of Egypt. "No one is to appear before me empty-handed." (Exodus 23:15 NIV)

"For the Lord your God is bringing you into a good land—a land with brooks, streams, and deep springs gushing out into the valleys and hills; a land with wheat and barley, vines and fig trees, pomegranates, olive oil and honey; a land where bread will not be scarce and you will lack nothing; a land where the rocks are iron and you can dig copper out of the hills. When you have eaten and are satisfied, praise the Lord your God for the good land he has given you. Be careful that you do not forget the Lord your God, failing to observe his commands, his laws and his decrees that I am giving you this day. Otherwise, when you eat and are satisfied, when you build fine houses and settle down, and when your herds and flocks grow large and your silver and gold increase and all you have is multiplied, then your heart will become proud and you will forget the Lord your God, who brought you out of Egypt, out of the land of slavery… But remember the Lord your God, for it is he who gives you the ability to produce wealth, and so confirms his covenant, which he swore to your ancestors, as it is today." (Deuteronomy 8:7-14, 18 NIV)

"All these blessings will come on you and accompany you if you obey the Lord your God: You will be blessed in the city and blessed in the country. The fruit of your womb will be blessed, and the crops of your land and the young of your livestock—the calves of your herds and the lambs of your flocks. Your basket and your kneading trough will be blessed. You will be blessed when you come in and blessed when you go out. The Lord will grant that the enemies who rise up against you will be defeated before you. They will come at you from one direction but flee from you in seven. The Lord will send a blessing on your barns and on everything you put your hand to. The Lord your God will bless you in the land he is giving you." (Deuteronomy 28:2-8 NIV)

"The Lord will grant you abundant prosperity—in the fruit of your womb, the young of your livestock and the crops of your ground—in the land he swore to your ancestors to give you. The Lord will open the heavens, the storehouse of his bounty, to send rain on your land in season and to bless all the work of your hands. You will lend to many nations but will borrow from none. The Lord will make you the head, not the tail. If

you pay attention to the commands of the Lord your God that I give you this day and carefully follow them, you will always be at the top, never at the bottom." (Deuteronomy 28:11-13 NIV)

"Keep this Book of the Law always on your lips; meditate on it day and night, so that you may be careful to do everything written in it. Then you will be prosperous and successful." (Joshua 1:8 NIV)

"Bring the whole tithe into the storehouse, that there may be food in my house. Test me in this," says the Lord Almighty, "and see if I will not throw open the floodgates of heaven and pour out so much blessing that there will not be room enough to store it. I will prevent pests from devouring your crops, and the vines in your fields will not drop their fruit before it is ripe," says the Lord Almighty. "Then all the nations will call you blessed, for yours will be a delightful land," says the Lord Almighty." (Malachi 3:10-12 NIV)

"A good person leaves an inheritance for their children's children, but a sinner's wealth is stored up for the righteous." (Proverbs 13:22 NIV)

"The Lord is my shepherd, I lack nothing." (Psalm 23:1 NIV)

"The lions may grow weak and hungry, but those who seek the Lord lack no good thing." (Psalm 34:10 NIV)

"I was young and now I am old, yet I have never seen the righteous forsaken or their children begging bread." (Psalm 37:25 NIV)

"Give, and it will be given to you. A good measure, pressed down, shaken together and running over, will be poured into your lap. For with the measure you use, it will be measured to you." (Luke 6:38 NIV)

"So do not worry, saying, 'What shall we eat?' or 'What shall we drink?' or 'What shall we wear?' For the pagans run after all these things, and your heavenly Father knows that you need them. But seek first his kingdom and his righteousness, and all these things will be given to you as well." (Matthew 6:31-33 NIV)

"Heal the sick, raise the dead, cleanse those who have leprosy, drive out demons. Freely you have received; freely give." (Matthew 10:8 NIV)

"And my God will meet all your needs according to the riches of his glory in Christ Jesus." (Philippians 4:19 NIV)

"Jabez was more honorable than his brothers. His mother had named him Jabez, saying, "I gave birth to him in pain." Jabez cried out to the God of Israel, "Oh, that you would bless me and enlarge my territory! Let your hand be with me, and keep me from harm so that I will be free from pain." And God granted his request." (I Chronicles 4:9 NIV)

"On the first day of every week, each one of you should set aside a sum of money in keeping with your income, saving it up, so that when I come no collections will have to be made." (I Corinthians 16:2 NIV)

"Remember this: Whoever sows sparingly will also reap sparingly, and whoever sows generously will also reap generously. Each of you should give what you have decided in your heart to give, not reluctantly or under compulsion, for God loves a cheerful giver. And God is able to bless you abundantly, so that in all things at all times, having all that you need, you will abound in every good work." (II Corinthians 9:6-8 NIV)

"Dear friend, I pray that you may enjoy good health and that all may go well with you, even as your soul is getting along well." (III John 3:2 NIV)

Made in the USA
Monee, IL
04 November 2026

67352886R00015